A BRIEF HISTORY OF THE STAUNTON
AND
JAMES RIVER TURNPIKE [VIRGINIA]

Virginia Genealogical Society
Richmond, Virginia

Published With Permission from the

Virginia Transportation Research Council
(A Cooperative Organization Sponsored Jointly by the Virginia
Department of Transportation and
the University of Virginia)

HERITAGE BOOKS
2008

HERITAGE BOOKS
AN IMPRINT OF HERITAGE BOOKS, INC.

Books, CDs, and more—Worldwide

For our listing of thousands of titles see our website
at
www.HeritageBooks.com

Published 2008 by
HERITAGE BOOKS, INC.
Publishing Division
100 Railroad Avenue #104
Westminster, Maryland 21157

International Standard Book Number: 978-0-7884-3662-8

A BRIEF HISTORY OF THE STAUNTON AND JAMES RIVER TURNPIKE

by

Douglas Young
Student Assistant

The opinions, findings, and conclusions expressed in this report are those of the author
and not necessarily those of the sponsoring agencies.)

Virginia Highway & Transportation Research Council
(A Cooperative Organization Sponsored Jointly by the Virginia Department of
Highways & Transportation and
the University of Virginia)

Charlottesville, Virginia

May 1975
VHTRC 75-R59

Revised March 1980
Revised September 2003

Library of Congress Catalogue Card
No: 80-620005

FOREWORD

FOREWORD

Originally published in a limited edition in 1975 as a cooperative venture with Professor O.A. Gianniny of the School of Engineering and Applied Science of the University of Virginia, this publication was reprinted in 1976. The belief that this paper is a good example of what individuals in local historical groups could accomplish by the use of readily available resources has again caused its reissue.

From road orders available at the county courthouses, the published Acts of Assembly, the records of the Board of Public Works, Confederate Engineers Maps and those published by the Virginia Department of Highways & Transportation, similar brief histories and route maps can be constructed for most of the eighteenth-and nineteenth-century turnpikes in Virginia. The 1816-1902 records of the Board of Public Works, Virginia's coordinating body for internal improvements such as canals, railroads and turnpikes, are now available on microfilm, thanks to the efforts of Howard Newlon, Jr. of the Council and Donald Haynes of the Virginia State Library. Most of the Confederate maps are also available at either the State Library or the Virginia Historical Society in Richmond. Architectural surveys such as those available at the Virginia Historic Landmarks Commission and the School of Architecture at the University of Virginia can often provide additional information as to tollhouse and tavern locations along the routes. Fortunately, most of the turnpike routes are still in service as primary or secondary roads, thus simplifying the task of the amateur road historian as he explores the history of the roads we tend to take for granted in our day-to-day lives.

With turnpikes numbering in the hundreds, it is obvious that this work should be undertaken by individuals living in the communities through which they run. The magnitude of the project, as well as the necessity for on-site tracing of the original routes and their relationship to the political, social and economic development of the communities involved, places it well beyond the reach of government agencies and indicates the necessity for local direction of the effort. The Virginia Highway and Transportation Research Council anticipates the development of a program to encourage such efforts by individuals as well as local historical groups.

Nathaniel Mason Pawlett, M.A. (VIRG:),
Faculty Research Historian

PREFACE

This report was prepared to fulfill the requirements for the senior undergraduate thesis in the Humanities program of the University of Virginia's School of Engineering and Applied Science. Prof. O. A. Gianniny provided overall guidance.

This paper would not have been possible without the technical assistance of Howard H. Newlon, Jr. and Nathaniel Mason Pawlett of the Virginia Highway and Transportation Research Council, whose help is deeply appreciated. Appreciation is also expressed to H. M. Shaver of the Virginia Department of Highways and Transportation who furnished air photos and other information.

ABSTRACT

After the Revolutionary War an increasing number of settlers crossed the Blue Ridge Mountains of Virginia to live in the Shenandoah Valley and Trans-Allegheny Region. With this increase in population, a means of transportation connecting the east and west was needed. Therefore, in 1825, the General Assembly appropriated $50,000 for the construction of a road connecting Staunton and Scottsville on the James River.

Construction of the 43 ½ mile dirt road started in 1825 and the first tolls were collected in May 1826. The road went east from Staunton to Waynesboro, over the Blue Ridge Mountains at Rockfish Gap, through the Ragged Mountains at Israel's Gap, and then on to Scottsville. The road passed through many low and miry spots from the Blue Ridge to Israel's Gap, making it almost impossible for wagons to pass during wet seasons.

Although the turnpike carried much traffic, the directors of the company and members of Virginia's State Board of Public Works continually suggested that the road be Macadamized in order to ensure its year-round use.

The General Assembly reorganized the company and increased its capital stock through acts in 1847 and 1849. The company had the option of either Macadamizing or planking the road. The latter was chosen and conversion was started in 1850. The early 1850's were the peak years of the turnpike, even though the road was not totally planked. The emergence of railroads and competition from a Macadamized road running from Staunton to Winchester cut deeply into the use of the turnpike and the road fell into disrepair, finally being referred to as the "mud turnpike". In 1860, the General Assembly made it lawful for Augusta and Albemarle Counties to purchase the turnpike, ending a part of Virginia's early turnpike system.

A BRIEF HISTORY OF THE
STAUNTON AND JAMES RIVER
TURNPIKE

by

Douglas Young
Student Assistant

INTRODUCTION

During the early nineteenth century the United States experienced a period of growth and expansion. To help meet needs occasioned by this growth, improved means of communication and transportation were established. Among these improvements were the construction of turnpikes. The period from 1800-1830 has, in fact, been termed by George Rogers Taylor as the "Turnpike Era".(1)

During this time, the state of Virginia was involved in the construction of many turnpikes. Among them was a road connecting Staunton and Scottsville, known as the Staunton and James River Turnpike. This report focuses on the history of this road and traces its life, mainly through the use of documents relating to it. Included is a brief discussion of the reasons for its construction and the factors that led to its eventual failure.

A description of the route in terms of modern roads and landmarks also is included. This section indicates the problems encountered during the construction and operation of the turnpike, and delineates the portions of the original route that are being used today.

Although this report is concerned with the history of a specific turnpike, in a general way, it reflects the formation and operation of Virginia turnpikes in the early nineteenth century.

THE NEED FOR A ROAD

Prior to the Revolutionary War, settlers on the western side of the Blue Ridge Mountains in Virginia were largely unconcerned with their lack of representation in the

Virginia legislature. After the war, however, thousands of settlers moved westward across the mountains and grew concerned about their lack of governmental representation. The lack of representation can be shown in the differences of population and the number of state representatives from each area at that time. The counties west of the Blue Ridge had a white population of 212,036 with only four state senators, while the east had a population of 162,717 and was represented by thirteen state senators. The Westerners were also in need of better means of communication, such as roads, canals, bridges and ferries. To these ends they organized a convention, held in 1816 in Staunton, to help make their grievances known in Richmond.(2)

Political pressure and the possible loss of the Shenandoah Valley trade to Baltimore or Philadelphia were key factors leading to Eastern Virginia's support for the establishment of internal improvement programs in the early nineteenth century.(3) In the same year that the Staunton convention was held, the General Assembly created a fund .for internal improvements and a Board of Public Works to administer it.

Foremost among the projects undertaken by the Board of Public Works was the improvement of the navigation of the James River. The project, known as the James River and Kanawha Canal, improved the river westward to Buchanan. With this improvement Scottsville became a busy trading town on the James River.(4) As the prospects of attracting trade from the western side of the Blue Ridge grew, a road connecting Scottsville and Staunton seemed a potentially profitable venture.

FORMATION

Therefore on February 13, 1818, the General Assembly of Virginia passed a bill authorizing the construction of a turnpike connecting Staunton to Scott's landing on the James River with a subscription of $200,000. The company formed, known as the Staunton and James River Turnpike Company, had the right to designate the point on the James River for the road's termination.(5) This bill was revived on March 8, 1824, and mentioned that the state would finance two-fifths of the $200,000 with the remaining three-fifths to be paid by private subscribers.(6) Later, on February 12, 1825, the act was further amended to change the subscription to $50,000 to be financed in the same manner as prescribed in the 1824 act. The act further stipulated that the road be "constructed ...thirty feet in width, duly graduated according to the provisions of the general turnpike law, but need not be paved except where in the opinion of the commissioners appointed by the company it shall be deemed essentially necessary."(7)

After the private subscription had been collected, the General Assembly passed a bill releasing $20,000 from the internal improvement fund to the turnpike company on February 24,1826.(8)

Although these acts established the Staunton and James River Turnpike, the idea for a road connecting the Blue Ridge and Scottsville had existed much earlier. On January 4, 1764, the General Assembly passed a bill authorizing Augusta County to collect up to £ 150 for the construction of a road over the Blue Ridge Mountains at Rockfish Gap.(9) In 1784 the General Assembly passed another bill for the general repair of this road.(10) The first document suggesting a road between the Blue Ridge and Scottsville was written in 1790. In that year the General Assembly authorized a lottery to raise £ 400 "to be applied towards paying the expenses as well as the damages incurred by cutting a road from Rockfish Gap to Nichol's and Scott's landing on the Fluvanna river in the county of Albemarle."(11) In the eighteenth century the present James River above Point of Fork was called the Rivanna River and the present Rivanna River was called the James.

This road was never constructed as the General Assembly passed a bill on Feb. 1, 1811, making it lawful to collect $60,000 in private subscription to open the road already established by law from Rockfish Gap to Scott's Ferry on the James River. The company was to be known as the Albemarle Turnpike Company, but it never received enough subscriptions to be formed.(12)

Although a road connecting the Blue Ridge and Scottsville didn't materialize in 1811, the Rockfish Gap Turnpike remained in use. The order books of Albemarle County mention that the turnpike commissioners appointed by the General Assembly were busy appointing people to superintend the road at that time.(13)

CONSTRUCTION

After the Act of 1826, construction began on the 43 ½ mile road. The turnpike followed a route from Staunton to Waynesboro, over the Blue Ridge Mountains at Rockfish Gap, through the Ragged Mountains at Israel's Gap, and then on to Scottsville. The route in many areas followed existing roads. Although construction of the entire road was not then completed, the first tolls for the turnpike were collected on May 15, 1826, on the completed Waynesboro-Staunton section.

After viewing the uncompleted road for the first time, Claude Crozet, state engineer of Virginia, described many faults in the construction. Among the problems were (1) the crest of the road was too high (15 inches higher than the edges), (2) the grade was too steep over the Blue Ridge Mountains (exceeding 5 ½ ° in some locations), and (3) from the base of the Blue Ridge eastward to Israel's Gap, it passed through many low and miry places. Crozet also expressed his dissatisfaction with the section from Staunton to Waynesboro because too much attention had been given to the straightness of the road instead of conforming it to the rolling terrain. The importance of this road was shown in Crozet's report, "This turnpike will greatly benefit the trade of the upper country, and it is reasonable to expect that it will add much to the revenue of the James river navigation, about eighty miles of which, will now substitute the same distance of land transportation over a very bad road."(14)

The cost of construction varied for different sections of the road. From Staunton to Waynesboro, a distance of about 11 miles, the road cost $700 per mile; across the Blue Ridge, a distance of about 5 miles, costs were $5,500 per mile; and the remaining 27 miles to Scottsville cost $685 per mile.(15)

THE EARLY YEARS

The return statement of the first year for the turnpike in November 1827 showed that the company had collected $2,085 in tolls and was able to declare a six percent dividend to its stockholders. During the first year of operation, the company decided to purchase the unexpired term of the Rockfish Gap Turnpike Company and appropriated almost one-half of the tolls collected to do so. The company hired two hands and a superintendent for the purpose of keeping the road in repair that year.(16)

Engineer Crozet was later able to view the entire completed road and again in his report stated the many problems with the road. Among the difficulties he mentioned were that much of the road had to be capped with stone and the grade was still much too steep in some sections. Crozet went on to say that "Although this turnpike is not so good as it might have been, it will nevertheless be one of the best roads in the State, when miry places in it shall have been made firm by the super-addition of a bed of broken stone."(17)

William Kinney, Jr. of Staunton, president of the turnpike, describes the road in the 1830 annual report as a 43 ½ mile road connecting Staunton and Scottsville with toll gates erected at Christian's Creek, Rockfish Gap, Israel's Gap, Garland's store, and Scottsville. Kinney's report further described the road as being 22 feet wide with timber cleared an additional 14 feet on each side, and with bridges of some extent crossing Christian's Creek, the South Fork of Mechum River, and the South Fork of the Hardware River. Describing the use of the road, the report states, "The principal object contemplated by the construction of this road in the first place is believed to have been to furnish to the planters and farmers of a good part of Albemarle, Nelson, and Augusta, a more convenient and easy communication to James River at Scottsville. Since the improvement has been made, it has drawn to it a considerable quantity of produce from the counties of Rockingham, Rockbridge, Bath, and Pendeleton. It is also traveled by many wagons, carriages, and horsemen destined for Richmond."(18)

The poor construction of the road made it very difficult to keep open for the collection of tolls throughout the year. Joseph Brown, president of the turnpike, points out in the annual report of 1831, "In consequence of the unusual quantity of snow and rain, which fell during the last winter and spring (we) were compelled to keep the gates open nearly all the winter and early part of the spring."(19) The term "open gates" refers to not collecting tolls due to the poor condition of the road. He also alludes to Crozet's remarks towards making the road more permanent. "The directors confidently believe that as soon as the road can be made of that permanent character, so as to ensure the safe and certain passage of market wagons at all seasons of the year, no improvement in the state of a similar character, will yield a better profit to the stockholders, and at the same time diffuse greater benefits to that portion of the community, who find it the most convenient road to market."(20)

DEVELOPMENT OF A PERMANENT SURFACE

The use of the turnpike continued to increase and Brown notes in his 1832 report, "On a comparison of the tolls of this and the preceding years, it will be found that they are gradually increasing, and will, it is believed, continue to increase for several years."(21) The hope of making the road permanent is again mentioned by Brown in the same report,. "The directors entertain no doubt, that if this road was M'Adamized or gravelled so as to make it a safe and firm carriage way for market waggons at all seasons of the year, that its stock would become more valuable, and the work itself diffuse more general benefit to the country as a market road, than any other of the same extent in Virginia."(22)

To try to make a more lasting surface on the road, the turnpike let out sections of the road to contractors for general repair and gravelling. Each contractor was to gravel one-fourth mile for every 5 miles he was responsible for, which resulted in the paving of just 2 ¼ miles per year. (23) In 1834 this procedure was changed; the company hired a general agent for $500 who acted as treasurer and secretary and was authorized to hire from 15 to 25 hands to carry out repair work on the road.(24)

No dividends were declared in 1834. The reason for this was than money was raised to try an experiment in improving the condition of the road. The plan was to bury timber and form a ramp to make it easier for wagons to pass on and off the road.(25) The experiment was not satisfactory to the stockholders and the money appropriated was used to put the road into good condition by renewing bridges and culverts and opening side ditches. Charles Shaw, principal engineer, comments on the experiment as a plan too ridiculous to mention.(26)

The general condition of the road deteriorated the following years as evidenced by statements in the annual reports. The directors felt that the state should appropriate more money to the turnpike, or that a new means of transportation, namely the railroad, should provide the transportation between Scottsville and Staunton.

A survey for the possibility of a railroad connecting the two towns was conducted in 1835 by Charles Shaw and John Conty, maps of which are in the Virginia State Library, Richmond, Virginia.

The following excerpts taken from various annual reports show the feelings of the directors: "... the stockholders look forward to the day, not very far distant, when this turnpike will give way to a railroad. It is, therefore, considered unwise to be expending all the tolls on making partial improvements."(27) "Public opinion in this part of the country requires some better mode of getting to market than this road will ever afford, and we thought our policy ought to be to keep this road in sufficient order to receive tolls without attempting any expensive improvements, and divide something to the stockholders."(28) "...It will be the object of the directors to keep the road at as little expense as possible believing that the present must some day give way to a more permanent road."(29)

In 1841, J. Smith, (probably Joseph Smith of Smith's Folly near Staunton), president of the turnpike, expressed concern on losing trade to Baltimore by the Valley Road through Winchester unless the road was macadamized. "The road at this time is in better order from Staunton to Scottsville than it has been for many years, but owing to its manner of construction we have no right calculating on its long continuance, for at the very time it is most needed by the agriculturist (winter), it becomes almost impassable, and unless some more permanent mode is adopted for its construction, we much fear that the greater part of the trade and produce of the valley will be diverted from its proper channel (the James River canal) and drawn to Baltimore through the M'Adamized road down the valley to Winchester."(30) Smith also mentions the possibility of selling the stockholders' three-fifths to the state, "... the state should become the owner of the entire stock by purchasing from the stockholders their three-fifths, at a fair value, and then either construct a railroad to Scottsville, or change the present improvement into a M'Adamized road."(31)

The condition of the road became so bad that no work could be done on it during the winter months. "It has been found by experience that it is useless and unnecessary to put hands on the road earlier than the first of March owing to the peculiar character of the soil over which the road passes. If between the 1st of January and the 1st of March it should become absolutely necessary to do anything, a few hands are temporarily hired."(32)

The poor construction of the road and its effect on trade from the Valley is again pointed out in the 1844 report of the Board of Public Works, "This road ...is not at all calculated to accommodate the great trade that once took that route, but which owing to the attractions of a rival improvement (the Valley turnpike), since made of much superior character, has been mostly diverted from it. Its original location was not only injudicious in many instances, as it regarded the choice of route, but the nature of the soil or material throughout which the location was directed was frequently most unsuitable — consequences of the latter fault is, that during the season of the year when the business of the road is usually heaviest, the road becomes almost impassable for wagons, even with light loads. As soon therefore as the valley turnpike between Staunton and Winchester was constructed on the Macadam principle farmers were enabled to carry so much heavier loads with the same teams, and at so much less cost of time, expense, and wear and tear of property that the greater portion of that produce which once helped to build up the city of Richmond, now contribute to increase the growing importance of Baltimore."(33) The report continues, "More attention appears to be paid to the interests of the Staunton and James River turnpike than has been usual for some years; but the day of its prosperity has passed away, as no road of so imperfect a character, however well managed, can compete with the superior advantages held out by a Macadamized road."(34)

STUDY ON MACADAMIZED ROAD

During the middle 1840's much attention was given to the possibility of Macadamizing the entire turnpike. In 1844 a study was conducted by Edwin M. Taylor on the costs and benefits to be derived from the paving of the turnpike. The route Taylor proposed had a maximum grade of 3 ½° and a total length of 46 miles, about 2 miles longer than the original road. The road was to have a width of 22 feet and be covered with stones at a width of 17 feet. The stone covering was to be 9 inches thick. The projected cost for paving the entire road was $169,793. Taylor went into great detail in comparing an improved road between Staunton and Scottsville to that of the Valley road. Taylor's estimates were based on ten cents per wagon per horse per section for a trip to market and five cents per section for the return trip. Thus, for a typical six-horse wagon the toll would amount to three dollars to Scottsville and one and one-half dollars for the return trip. Part of Taylor's comparison of the two routes is listed below.(35)

Transportation of a barrel of flour from Staunton to Baltimore		96 cents
Transportation of a barrel of flour from Staunton to Scottsville	29	
Forwarding per barrel (can be afforded) at Scottsville	5	
Freight per barrel can be reduced a little on the canal so as to make the sum of the freight and toll from Scottsville to Richmond amount to	34	
Transportation of one barrel of flour from Staunton to Richmond		68 cents
'Difference in favour of the latter route		28 cents

Estimated annual income derived from the road was also computed.

115,000 barrels of flour at 35 barrels to a 6 horse wagon will require	3286	
20,000 cwt. of sundries will require	300	
	3568 wagons @ $	10,758
Same wagons returning generally laden with merchandize, plaster, salt, & c., will be	3596 wagons @ $1.50	5,379
Toll from stages and private travel,		2,000
	Total receipts	18,137
Deduct for cost of repairs, salaries of Superintendent, and tollgate keepers, and incidental expenses		5,000

Net annual income $13,137

Taylor's report also mentions the relation of the turnpike to the James River and Kanawha Canal. "The Staunton and James River turnpike was once (the canal's) most valuable tributary; and it is evident from the great and rapid decrease in the amount of produce now brought to Scottsville, as compared with that formerly delivered there, that the canal cannot much longer look to the quarter for any important contributions to its income."(36) Taylor's report was very favorable to the paving of the turnpike both to increase trade to Richmond and also to help the James River and Kanawha Canal.

Further support for Macadamizing the road came from William Hamilton, superintendent of the Staunton and Parkersburg Road. In the 30th annual report, Hamilton states his mistake in voting in 1844 against a bill to Macadamize the Staunton and James River turnpike. After passing over the road and seeing 50 wagons driving through stiff mud, able to travel only 10 miles a day, he recognized the importance of the road and wanted the Board of Public Works to know his change in attitude towards paving of the road.(37)

The operation of the road continued during the period as it had before, with the addition of gravel to the road in low, marshy areas. Optimism among the directors must have developed as in the 1847 report they expressed the opinion that the road was starting to improve year by year.(38) However, Macadamizing the road is mentioned as a possible improvement if the railroad does not expand. "Where it possible to have this road relocated in part and M'Adamized, it could not be otherwise than a source of great benefit to the farmer, as well as profit to the stockholders, the extension of the Louisa railroad not withstanding."(39). The Louisa Railroad was chartered in 1836 and was a feeder line for the Richmond, Fredericksburg, and Potomac Railroad serving Louisa County. The railroad was eventually extended westward through Charlottesville and was later known as the Virginia Central and then the Chesapeake and Ohio.(40, 41)

REORGANIZATION OF THE TURNPIKE

A major turn of events happened to the company when it was reorganized by acts in 1847 and an amendment in 1849. The headquarters of the company were moved from Staunton to Scottsville, and the capital stock was increased to $84,000 for the purpose of Macadamizing the road. This bill was amended in March 1849 so that the company could have the option to construct either a plank or Macadamized surface.(42) The company chose a plank road and construction and surveying started in 1849.

THE PLANK ROAD

At that time plank roads were being constructed across the country. Very simply they were wooden roads constructed on a graded earthwork. The cost of construction per mile of plank road varied from $1,500 to $1,800 compared to $3,500 to $4,000 for Macadamized surface.(43) The annual report for the company in 1850 states that the plank had been placed on the road for five or six miles and that about two miles were completed. At that time the directors thought that the work was progressing in a manner to ensure a speedy completion.(44)

In the 37th annual report, it was noted that $51,754.61 had been spent on the construction of the new road. William M. Wade, probably of Scottsville, secretary of the turnpike company, writes, "This improvement was originally designed to reach the eastern base of the Blue Ridge at Brooksville, but only 10 miles of the road had been finished, leaving 15 miles uncompleted." (45) Although the road was not totally planked, the early 1850's were the peak years for the turnpike. A correspondent of the Southern Planter reported that he had seen 70 mountain wagons waiting to load in Scottsville.(46) Although the road was in heavy use, the general condition of the company was in confusion as shown by the 37th annual report. "It is impossible to give a satisfactory report of the state and condition of the road, from the fact that no regular books have been heretofore kept and the affairs of the company consequently in great confusion."(47) Reports of the following years clearly illustrate this disorder as there is a $4,000 error in the listed value for the capital stock of the company.

THE CLOSING YEARS

The remaining reports for the Staunton and James River turnpike contain little information except for the basic financial statements. From the returns, it appears that the road was hardly used in 1860 as only $293.45 was collected. At that time $80,190.64 had been spent in the construction of the plank road. A report on plank roads in general was made by Thomas H. DeWitt, president of the Board of Public Works, in 1858. The report states that the permanency of plank roads is very discouraging, and not enough income can be derived from the road to keep the planks in repair.(48) This proved to be an exact description of conditions on the Staunton and James River turnpike.

The downfall of the turnpike closely follows the emergence and acceptance of rail transportation in Virginia. Trade through Scottsville shrank as both the Virginia Central and the Orange and Alexandria railroads bypassed Scottsville. The Virginia Central is now known as the Chesapeake and Ohio. The route taken by the railroad westward bypassed Scottsville in favor of going through Charlottesville. Service began in 1849 to Shadwell, five miles east of Charlottesville, and extended westward through the Blue Ridge to Staunton in 1858.(49) The Orange and Alexandria Railroad was chartered in 1847 and went from Alexandria through Charlottesville to Lynchburg. The railroad is now known as the Southern Railroad.(50)

The plank road began deteriorating faster than it could be repaired and became known as the 'mud turnpike'.(51) Finally on March 31, 1860, the General Assembly passed a bill making it lawful for Augusta and Albemarle Counties to purchase the Staunton and James River turnpike, thus ending an early part of Virginia's transport system.(52)

CONCLUSIONS

Although the Staunton and James River turnpike was a key link between Staunton and Scottsville for many years, the potential of the road was never fully developed, due to a lack of money, lack of foresight in management, and the emergence of rail transportation.

Many times during the existence of the turnpike, directors of the company and members of the Board of Public Works suggested that funds be raised to Macadamize the road to ensure passage of vehicles at any time of year. Due to a lack of money, brought about by the opinions of certain directors who held that no improvements should be made on the road except to maintain its general level of upkeep, the Macadamizing program was never undertaken.

The completion of the Macadamized Valley Turnpike coupled with the emergence of rail transportation, had begun to take effect on the operations of the turnpike when an attempt to modernize the road through planking was initiated in the 1850's. Although plank roads had yet to be proven, the company chose this method of surface improvement over the Macadam principle. Thus the decline in trade and the deteriorating condition of the road led to the dissolution of the company.

Although the improvement of planking was designed to upgrade the road, the experimental nature of this method proved to be too little, too late, and inadequate. If the road had been Macadamized at the onset, the importance of the Staunton and James River turnpike may well have been greater than the effect we see today.

THE ROAD TODAY

With aerial photographs and maps supplied by the Virginia Department of Highways and Transportation, it is possible to trace what appears to be the route of the Staunton and James River Turnpike. The approximate route is indicated in figure 1. The turnpike route can still be closely followed on present roads by many of the landmarks that were part of the original road.

Starting in Staunton, the turnpike followed the present U. S. Route 250 eastward across Christian's Creek towards Waynesboro. This area is heavily built up and it is very difficult to locate anything that looks like the original route. Once through Waynesboro, the turnpike continued on U. S. 250 up the western side of the

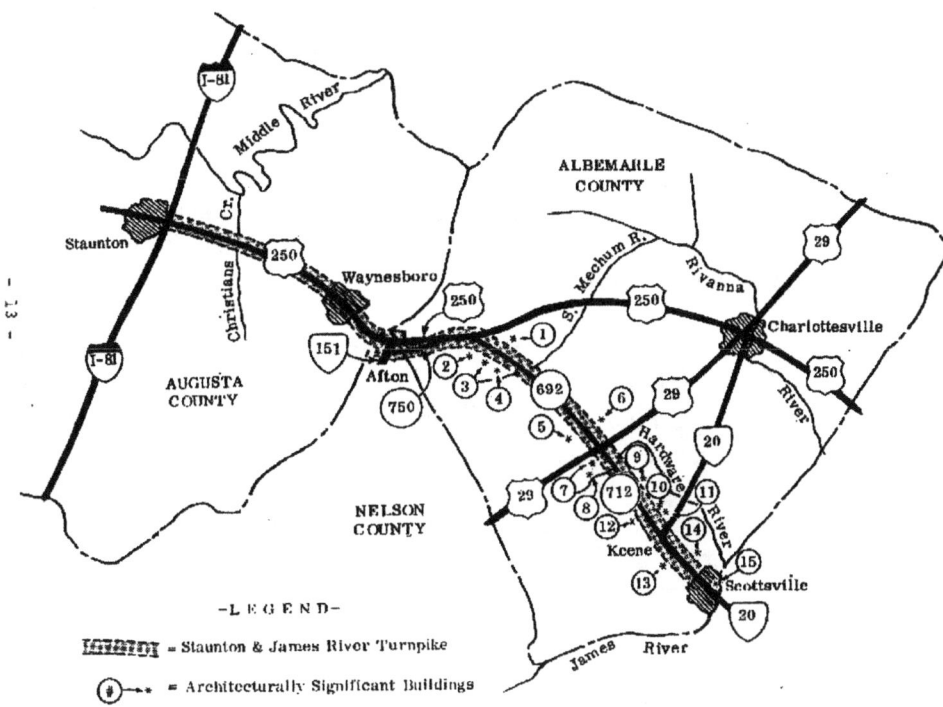

Figure 1. Staunton and James River Turnpike: Present Day Routes.

Blue Ridge Mountains to Afton Mountain. Again this area is highly developed and any traces of the original route are gone due to the construction of Interstate 64 and improvements to U. S. 250. On the east side of the mountain however, what appears to be the original route can be taken by getting off U. S. 250 and going through the village of Afton to Route 750. This road has several switchbacks as it proceeds down the face of the mountain. The road joins Route 250 for a short distance and then cuts off at Route 692. This road goes through Batesville and then across U. S. Route 29 at Cross Roads. The road here becomes Route 712, which follows what appears to be the original route through North and South Garden to Keene. At this point it joins Route 20 and follows it southward into Scottsville.

The road today passes many buildings that were there during the original use of the road. Among the extant buildings that served the original road are toll houses and taverns. Three are shown in Figures 2-4. One tavern is located at Cross Roads (on the western side of Route 29); a toll house is at Garland's Store, located at the intersection of Route 712 and Route 631; and another tavern is in Scottsville. A detailed history of the architecture along the road is being compiled by Dr. K. E. Lay, a professor of architecture at the University of Virginia.

Figure 2. Crossroads Tavern (692 & U.S. 29).

Figure 3. Garland's Store (712 & 631).

Figure 4. Tavern (Scottsville).

The following buildings from the period of the road may be seen along the routes today. The numbers correspond to the following map.

1. Port-A-Ferry (north side of 692 between 691 and 637)

2. Blue Hill Farm (off 691 south of 692)

3. Wavertree (south of 692 between 691 and 637)

4. Foster House and Barn (south of 692 east of 637)

5. Sutherland Brick Barn (south side of 692 west of U. S. 29)

6. Cross Roads Tavern (north side of 692 west of U. S. 29, see Figure 1)

7. Mill (south side of 712 east of Southern Railroad)

8. Sunnybrook (north of 712 east of North Garden)

9. Garland's Store (northwest corner of 712 and 631, see Figure 2)

10. Alberene Church (corner of 712 and 655)

11. Estoutevil1e (north side of 712, east of 627)

12. Enniscorthy (south of 712 on west side of 627)

13. G1endower Millhouse (west side of 20, north of 713)

14. Fairview (east side of 20, north of Scottsvile)

15. Tavern (Scottsville, see Figure 3)

The pictures and information were supplied by Dr. Lay.

FOOTNOTES

1. George Rogers Taylor, <u>The Transportation Revolution 1815-1860</u>, Harper and Row, N.Y., 1951, p. 16.

2. Virginius Dabney, <u>Virginia, The New Dominion</u>, Doubleday, Garden City, N.Y., 1971, p. 213.

3. Howard Newlon, Jr., "Backsights", Bulletin, Virginia Department of Highways and Transportation, Sept. 1974, p. 12.

4. Virginia Moore, <u>Scottsville on the James</u>, Jarman Press Charlottesville, Va. 1969, p. 56.

5. Acts Passed at a General Assembly, 1818, pp. 132-133.

6. Acts Passed at a General Assembly, 1824, pp. 68-69.

7. Acts Passed at a General Assembly, 1825, p. 65.

8. Acts Passed at a General Assembly, 1826, pp. 66-67.

9. <u>Henings Statutes at Large</u>, Vol. 8, pp. 16-17.

10. <u>Henings Statutes at Large</u>, Vol. 11, pp. 429-430.

11. Acts Passed at a General Assembly, 1790, p. 32.

12. Acts Passed at a General Assembly, 1811, pp. 22-27.

13. Nathaniel Mason Pawlett, "Albemarle County Road Orders 1783-1816", Order book 1811-1813, p. 88 & p. 146.

14. Board of Public Works, 11th Annual Report, pp. 87-89.

15. Board of Public Works, 11th Annual Report, p. 89.

16. Board of Public Works, 12th Annual Report, p. 217.

17. Board of Public Works, 12th Annual Report, p. 336.

18. Board of Public Works, 15th Annual Report, p. 218.

19. Board of Public Works, 16th Annual Report, p. 361.

20. Board of Public Works, 16th Annual Report, pp. 361-362.

21. Board of Public Works, 17th Annual Report, p. 62.

22. Board of Public Works, 17th Annual Report, p. 63.

23. Board of Public Works, 16th Annual Report, p. 361.

24. Board of Public Works, 19th Annual Report, p. 486.

25. Board of Public Works, 19th Annual Report, p. 486.

26. Board of Public Works, 20th Annual Report, pp. 23-24.

27. Board of Public Works, 20th Annual Report, p. 145.

28. Board of Public Works, 21st Annual Report, p 344.

29. Board of Public Works, 22nd Annual Report, p. 328.

30. Board of Public Works, 26th Annual Report, p. 307.

31. Board of Public Works, 26th Annual Report, p. 307.

32. Board of Public Works, 28th Annual report, p. 47.

33. Board of Public Works, 28th Annual Report, p. 264.

34. Board of Public Works, 28th Annual Report, p. 264.

35. Memorial to the General Assembly, 1844, pp. 4-9.

36. Ibid, p. 4.

37. Board of Public Works, 30th Annual Report, p. 197.

38. Board of Public Works, 31st Annual Report, p. 309.

39. Board of Public Works, 33rd Annual Report, p. 467.

40. Moore, Scottsville on the James, p. 71.

41. Colonel William Couper, Claudius Crozet, Historical Publishing Co., Inc., Charlottesville, Va, 1936, pp. 127, 172.

42. Acts Passed at a General Assembly, 1849, pp. 114-115.

43. Howard Newlon, Jr., "Backsights", Bulletin, Virginia Department of Highways and Transportation, April 1974.

44. Board of Public Works, 35th Annual Report, p. 315.

45. Board of Public Works, 37th Annual Report, p. 71.

46. Moore, Scottsville on the James, p. 72.

47. Board of Public Works, 37th Annual Report, p. 71.

48. Board of Public Works, 43rd Annual Report.

49. Couper, Claudius Crozet, pp. 127, 172.

50. Angus J. Johnston II, "Virginia Railroads in April 1861", Journal of Southern History, Vol. 23, Southern Historical Association, 1957.

51. Moore, Scottsville on the James, p. 73.

52. Acts Passed at a General Assembly, 1860.

BIBLIOGRAPHY

Acts Passed at a General Assembly of the Commonwealth of Virginia 1790, 1811, 1818, 1824, 1826, 1847, 1860 (Richmond, Va.)

Annual Reports of the Board of Public Works to the General Assembly of Virginia: 12th Annual Report through 45th Annual Report.

Couper, Colonel William, *Claudius Crozet*, Historical Publishing Co., Inc., Charlottesville, Va., 1936.

Dabney, Virginius, Virginia, *The New Dominion,* Doubleday, Garden City, N. Y., 1971.

Gillespie, N. M., *A Manual of the Principle and Practice of Road Making*, 4th ed., A. S. Barnes and Co., New York, 1851.

Hening, William Waller, *Statutes at Large of the Laws of Virginia*, Charlottesville, Va., 1969.

Jones, Newton, *Charlottesville and Albemarle County, 1819-1860*, University of Virginia doctoral dissertation, 1950.

Johnston, Angus J. II, "Virginia Railroads in April 1861," Journal of Southern History, Vol. 23, Southern Historical Assoc1at10n, 1957.

Moore, Virginia, *Scottsvil le on the James*, Jarman Press, Charl ottesville, Va., 1969.

Newlon, Howard H., Jr., "Backsights", various issues appearing in the Bulletin, Virginia Department of Highways and Transportation.

Pawlett, Nathaniel Mason, "Albemarle County Road Orders 1783-1816" typescript in preparation for publication by the Virginia Highway & Transportation Research Council as part of the appendix to "History of the Roads of Albemarle County, Virginia."

Peyton, J. Lewis, *History of Augusta County, Virginia*, Bridgewater, Va., 1953.

Roberts, Edward Graham, *The Roads of Virginia 1607-1840*, University of Virginia doctoral dissertation, 1950.

Taylor, George Rogers, *The Transportation Revolution, 1815-1860*, Harper & Row, New York, 1951.

Waddell, Joseph A., *Annals of Augusta County, Virginia, 1726-1871*, C. Russell Caldwell, Staunton, Va., 1902.

Woods, Edgar, *Albemarle County in Virginia*, Bridgewater, C. J. Carrier Co., 1964.